Simple Guide to jQuery

Practical Guide

V. Telman

Copyright © 2024

Guide to jQuery

1. Introduction to jQuery

JavaScript has evolved tremendously over the years, enhancing the capabilities of web applications and providing an interactive experience for users. Amid this evolution, jQuery emerged as a powerful and influential library that simplifies script writing for HTML document manipulation, event handling, and animation. This introduction aims to provide a comprehensive overview of jQuery, its benefits, key features, and setup processes. This information will serve not only as a starting point for beginners but also as a refresher for seasoned developers.

What is jQuery?

jQuery is an open-source JavaScript library that simplifies the process of handling events, manipulating the Document Object Model (DOM), and executing AJAX calls. Released in 2006 by John Resig, jQuery was created with the goal of making it easier for developers to write and maintain JavaScript in their web applications. Its syntax is designed to allow developers to write less code to achieve more functionality, thereby increasing productivity and reducing development time.

By offering a concise and consistent API, jQuery aims to minimize discrepancies among web browsers, allowing developers to focus on creating rich, interactive web applications with less concern about compatibility issues. With its extensive plugin architecture, jQuery also allows easy extension of its capabilities, making it an adaptable choice for both simple and complex web projects.

Why Use jQuery?

There are several compelling reasons to consider using jQuery in your web development projects. Here are just a few of the most significant:

1. **Cross-Browser Compatibility**: jQuery handles many of the cross-browser inconsistencies that developers often face. This means you can write code that will work consistently across major browsers without needing extensive conditional statements.

2. **Simple Syntax**: jQuery's syntax is simple and intuitive, which makes it accessible to both beginner and experienced developers. It abstracts complex tasks into fewer lines of code, allowing developers to accomplish tasks with minimal effort.

3. **DOM Manipulation**: One of jQuery's key features is its ability to manipulate the DOM easily. Developers can select, modify, or remove elements in the document, as well as create new elements with relative ease.

4. **Animation and Effects**: jQuery offers built-in methods for creating animations and transitions. Developers can easily add effects like fading, sliding, and custom animations to web elements, enhancing the user experience.

5. **Event Handling**: jQuery streamlines event handling with a unified method for attaching event handlers to elements. This allows developers to implement interactions such as clicks, hovers, and keyboard events straightforwardly.

6. **AJAX Support**: jQuery makes it easier to create asynchronous HTTP requests, allowing for dynamic content loading without refreshing the entire page. This feature is essential for modern web applications that require a seamless user experience.

7. **Extensive Plugin Ecosystem**: The jQuery community is vast and active, producing thousands of plugins that can extend the library's functionality. This means developers can find pre-built solutions for a wide variety of tasks, from lightbox effects to complex user interfaces.

Quick Overview of jQuery Features

Here's a brief overview of some of the fantastic features jQuery offers:

- **Selectors**: jQuery's powerful selector engine allows you to select DOM elements based on various criteria, such as tag name, class, ID, attributes, and more, making it easier to manipulate elements.

- **Chaining**: jQuery allows multiple

methods to be called on the same jQuery object in a single line, enabling a clean and fluid coding style. For example, you can combine DOM manipulation, event handling, and animations in one call.

- **Utilities**: jQuery includes utility functions, such as `$.each()`, for iterating over collections, `$.extend()` for merging objects, and `$.ajax()` for handling asynchronous requests efficiently.

- **Effects and Animations**: Built-in methods such as `.fadeIn()`, `.slideUp()`, and `.animate()` enable developers to create dynamic effects with a simple method call.

- **Callbacks and Promises**: jQuery supports callbacks for handling asynchronous operations and Promises for more complex asynchronous workflows, enabling a more structured approach to handling events.

- **AJAX Methods**: jQuery provides an array of AJAX methods (`$.get()`, `$.post()`, `$.ajax()`) that simplify sending and receiving data from servers, making it easier to build interactive applications.

Setting Up jQuery in Your Project

Getting started with jQuery is a straightforward process, involving just a few steps to include the library in your project. There are two primary methods for setting up jQuery: using a Content Delivery Network (CDN) or downloading the library for local hosting.

Including jQuery via CDN

Using a CDN to include jQuery is the most common and recommended approach, primarily due to its simplicity and effectiveness. Here are detailed steps to include jQuery via CDN:

1. **Choose a CDN**: There are several CDNs available for hosting jQuery, including Google, Microsoft, and CDNJS. A popular choice is Google's CDN.

2. **Include a Script Tag**: To include jQuery in your web project, simply add a

`<script>` tag in the `<head>` section of your HTML document or before the closing `</body>` tag. Here is an example of using Google's CDN:

```html
<!DOCTYPE html>
<html lang="en">
<head>
    <meta charset="UTF-8">
    <meta name="viewport" content="width=device-width, initial-scale=1.0">
    <title>Your Project</title>
    <script src="https://ajax.googleapis.com/ajax/libs/jquery/3.6.0/jquery.min.js"></script>
  </head>
  <body>
    <!-- Your content here -->
    <script>
      $(document).ready(function(){
        console.log("jQuery is working!");
      });
    </script>
  </body>
</html>
```

```

3. **Test Your Setup**: After adding the script tag, open your webpage in the browser, and check the Console (using Developer Tools) to ensure that jQuery is loaded correctly. You can do this by typing `jQuery` or `$` and pressing Enter; it should return the function definition instead of an error.

### Downloading and Hosting jQuery Locally

Alternatively, you may prefer to host jQuery locally. This means downloading the library file and serving it with your application. Here's how:

1. **Download jQuery**: Visit the official jQuery website ([jquery.com](jquery.com)) and navigate to the download section. There you can choose to download the minified version for production and the uncompressed version for development.

2. **Save the File**: After downloading, save the jQuery file to your project directory, preferably in a folder called `js` or `scripts`.
```

3. **Include the Script in Your HTML**: Update your HTML file to reference the downloaded jQuery file. Use a relative path in the `<script>` tag as shown below:

```html
<!DOCTYPE html>
<html lang="en">
<head>
    <meta charset="UTF-8">
    <meta name="viewport" content="width=device-width, initial-scale=1.0">
    <title>Your Project</title>
    <script src="js/jquery-3.6.0.min.js"></script>
  </head>
  <body>
    <!-- Your content here -->
    <script>
      $(document).ready(function(){
        console.log("jQuery is working!");
      });
    </script>
  </body>
</html>
```

```

4. **Test Your Local Setup**: As with the CDN setup, open your webpage in the browser and verify that jQuery loads correctly.

## Conclusion

In summary, jQuery is a valuable tool that simplifies many aspects of web development by providing a cohesive and elegant way to interact with the DOM, manage events, and facilitate AJAX calls, among other features. Its extensive support and large community have made it a staple in web programming. Setting it up is effortless, whether you choose to use a CDN or host it locally, making jQuery accessible to all developers, regardless of experience level. With these foundational concepts, you'll be well-equipped to begin exploring the powerful functionalities jQuery has to offer.
```

2. Basic Concepts in jQuery

jQuery is a powerful library in JavaScript that helps to simplify HTML document manipulation, event handling, animating, and Ajax interactions for rapid web development. In this comprehensive overview, we will delve into some foundational concepts in jQuery, including understanding the Document Object Model (DOM), jQuery syntax and selectors, and jQuery objects and methods.

Understanding the DOM (Document Object Model)

The Document Object Model (DOM) is a programming interface for web documents. It represents the structure of a document as a tree of objects, where each object corresponds to a part of the document, such as elements, attributes, and text nodes. In a web context, the DOM allows scripts to update the content, structure, and style of a document dynamically.

Key Points about the DOM:

1. **Tree Structure**: The DOM organizes the elements of a web page in a hierarchical structure. The document itself is the root node, and every HTML element is considered a node in this tree. Child nodes can have their own children, representing nested structures.

2. **Nodes and Objects**: In the DOM, there are different types of nodes:
   - **Element Nodes**: These represent HTML elements (e.g., `<div>`, `<p>`, `<a>`).
   - **Text Nodes**: These represent the text inside an element.
   - **Attribute Nodes**: These represent attributes of elements (e.g., `class`, `id`).

3. **Manipulating the DOM**: Using JavaScript (and jQuery, which is built on JavaScript), you can dynamically manipulate the DOM. This includes adding, removing, or modifying elements and their attributes on the fly, responding to user interactions, and more.

jQuery Syntax and Selectors

jQuery is known for its succinct syntax that allows developers to write less code to achieve more functionality. A key element of this syntax is the use of selectors to find and manipulate DOM elements effectively. Selectors can be broadly categorized into two types: CSS selectors and jQuery selectors.

1. CSS Selectors

CSS selectors are used to select elements based on their attributes, classes, IDs, and other properties. jQuery leverages CSS selector syntax, which means you can use familiar selectors to access DOM elements.

Common CSS Selectors
- `*` (Universal Selector): Select all elements.
- `#id`: Select an element with a specific ID.
- `.class`: Select all elements with a specific class.
- `element`: Select all elements of a specific type (e.g., `div`, `p`).
- `element.class`: Select all elements of a specific type with a specific class.
- `[attribute=value]`: Select elements with a specific attribute and value.

2. jQuery Selectors

In addition to CSS selectors, jQuery introduces specific selectors that optimize DOM selection and manipulation.

jQuery Selectors Overview:
- **ID Selectors**: `$('#id')` selects the element with the provided ID.
- **Class Selectors**: `$('.class')` selects all elements with the provided class name.
- **Element Selectors**: `$('element')` selects all instances of the specified element type.
- **Attribute Selectors**:
  - `$('input[name="username"]')` selects input elements with the name attribute set to "username".
  - `$('a[href="http://example.com"]')` selects anchor elements with a specific href value.

Example of jQuery Selectors:
```javascript
// Select a single element by ID
$('#myElement').css('color', 'red');

// Select all paragraphs and change their font size
$('p').css('font-size', '16px');
```

```javascript
// Select input fields of type text
$('input[type="text"]').val('Enter your name');
```

jQuery Objects and Methods

Once you've selected elements using jQuery selectors, the result is a jQuery object. This jQuery object contains all the functionality that jQuery provides for manipulating those selected elements.

jQuery Objects

A jQuery object is an array-like object that contains all the matched elements from the DOM. You can perform operations on these elements using jQuery methods.

Example:
```javascript
// Select paragraphs and store them in a jQuery object
var paragraphs = $('p');
```

jQuery Methods

jQuery provides a wide array of methods that can be invoked on jQuery objects. Here are some categories of common jQuery methods:

1. **Manipulation Methods**
- **`.html()`**: Get or set the HTML content of selected elements.
- **`.text()`**: Get or set the text content of selected elements.
- **`.val()`**: Get or set the value of form elements.
- **`.append()`**: Insert content at the end of selected elements.
- **`.prepend()`**: Insert content at the beginning of selected elements.
- **`.remove()`**: Remove selected elements from the DOM.

Example:
```javascript
// Change the HTML content of a div
$('#myDiv').html('<strong>New Content</strong>');

// Remove all paragraph elements
$('p').remove();
```

2. **CSS Methods**
- **`.css()`**: Get or set CSS properties of selected elements.
- **`.addClass()`**: Add a class to selected elements.
- **`.removeClass()`**: Remove a class from selected elements.
- **`.toggleClass()`**: Toggle a class on and off.

Example:
```javascript
// Change the background color of an element
$('#myElement').css('background-color', 'yellow');

// Add a class to all div elements
$('div').addClass('highlight');
```

3. **Event Methods**
- **`.on()`**: Attach an event handler to selected elements.
- **`.off()`**: Remove an event handler from selected elements.
- **`.click()`**: Attach a click event handler.
- **`.hover()`**: Attach mouse over and out

event handlers.

Example:
```javascript
// Attach a click event handler
$('#myButton').on('click', function() {
   alert('Button clicked!');
});

// Attach a hover event
$('#myDiv').hover(
   function() {
      $(this).css('color', 'blue');
   },
   function() {
      $(this).css('color', 'black');
   }
);
```

4. **Ajax Methods**
- **`.ajax()`**: Perform an asynchronous HTTP request.
- **`.get()`**: Simplified method for sending GET requests.
- **`.post()`**: Simplified method for sending POST requests.

Example:
```javascript
// Perform an AJAX GET request
$.get('https://api.example.com/data', function(response) {
   console.log(response);
});
```

In summary, jQuery is a powerful library for simplifying JavaScript programming, particularly in the context of DOM manipulation and event handling. Understanding the basics of the DOM, as well as mastering the jQuery syntax and its different selectors, forms a solid foundation for using jQuery effectively. Whether it's changing styles, handling user events, or performing AJAX calls, jQuery equips developers with an efficient way to enhance user interactivity and dynamic content on web pages. By leveraging jQuery objects and its rich multitude of methods, developers can create responsive and user-friendly applications with relative ease. This depth in jQuery understanding not only streamlines development but also allows for innovative approaches to front-end web development challenges.

3. Working with jQuery: An In-Depth Exploration of DOM Manipulation and CSS Modification

jQuery is a powerful, fast, and easy-to-use JavaScript library that simplifies HTML document traversal and manipulation, event handling, and Animation. It has become a staple in web development for its ability to streamline many tasks that involve working with the Document Object Model (DOM). In this comprehensive guide, we will delve into the various jQuery methods for DOM manipulation, CSS modification, and how to work with attributes and properties in a structured manner.

jQuery Methods for DOM Manipulation

jQuery provides several methods that make it easy to manipulate the DOM, allowing developers to interact with HTML elements seamlessly. Here, we will discuss key methods such as `.html()`, `.text()`, `.append()`, `.prepend()`, `.remove()`, and `.empty()`.

1. `.html()`

The `.html()` method is utilized to get or set the inner HTML content of an element. When called without arguments, it retrieves the current HTML content. When called with an argument, it sets the HTML content of the selected elements.

Example:

```javascript
// Getting HTML content
var content = $('#myElement').html();
console.log(content);

// Setting HTML content
$('#myElement').html('<p>New HTML Content</p>');
```

2. `.text()`

The `.text()` method is similar to `.html()`, but it deals specifically with plain text, disregarding any HTML tags. Like `.html()`, it can both retrieve and set text content.

Example:

```javascript
// Getting text content
var textContent = $('#myElement').text();
console.log(textContent);

// Setting text content
$('#myElement').text('New Text Content');
```

3. `.append()`

The `.append()` method is used to insert content (HTML or text) at the end of the selected elements. It can add one or more elements at a time.

Example:

```javascript
$('#myElement').append('<span>Appended Text</span>');
```

4. `.prepend()`

Conversely, the `.prepend()` method inserts content at the beginning of the selected elements. It is useful for adding new elements before existing content.

Example:

```javascript
$('#myElement').prepend('<span>Prepended Text</span>');
```

5. `.remove()`

The `.remove()` method removes the selected elements from the DOM entirely. This method is permanent, meaning the removed elements cannot be restored.

Example:

```javascript
$('#myElement').remove();
```

6. `.empty()`

The `.empty()` method removes all child elements of the selected elements but keeps the selected elements themselves intact. This is useful for clearing out content while maintaining the structure.

Example:

```javascript
$('#myElement').empty();
```

Modifying CSS with jQuery

jQuery also provides robust methods for modifying CSS properties and managing classes on elements. The methods discussed here include `.css()`, `.addClass()`, `.removeClass()`, and `.toggleClass()`.

1. `.css()`

The `.css()` method allows you to get or set CSS properties. Like previous methods, it functions by passing specific property names or an object containing multiple properties.

Example:

```javascript
// Getting CSS property
var color = $('#myElement').css('color');
console.log(color);

// Setting a single CSS property
$('#myElement').css('color', 'red');

// Setting multiple CSS properties
$('#myElement').css({
   'background-color': 'blue',
   'font-size': '16px'
});
```

2. `.addClass()`

The `.addClass()` method adds one or more specified classes to the selected elements. This is helpful for applying predefined styles or behaviors.

Example:

```javascript
$('#myElement').addClass('newClass');
```

3. `.removeClass()`

In contrast, the `.removeClass()` method removes one or more classes from the selected elements.

Example:

```javascript
$('#myElement').removeClass('oldClass');
```

4. `.toggleClass()`

The `.toggleClass()` method adds or removes a class from the selected elements based on whether it already exists. This is useful for toggling styles dynamically based on events.

Example:

```javascript
$('#myElement').toggleClass('active');
```

```

## Attributes and Properties

Manipulating attributes and properties is another essential part of DOM interaction. jQuery provides methods such as `.attr()`, `.prop()`, and `.val()` to facilitate this.

### 1. `.attr()`

The `.attr()` method is used to get or set attributes on the selected elements. This method can be useful for manipulating elements like images, links, and form fields.

#### Example:

```javascript
// Getting an attribute
var href = $('#myLink').attr('href');
console.log(href);

// Setting an attribute
$('#myLink').attr('href', 'https://new-url.com');
```
```

2. `.prop()`

The `.prop()` method operates similarly to `.attr()`, but it deals with properties rather than attributes. This distinction is important for elements like checkboxes or radio buttons.

Example:

```javascript
// Getting a property
var isChecked = $('#myCheckbox').prop('checked');
console.log(isChecked);

// Setting a property
$('#myCheckbox').prop('checked', true);
```

3. `.val()`

The `.val()` method is specifically designed for form elements, like input, select, and textarea. It retrieves the current value of the selected element or sets a new value.

Example:

```javascript
// Getting a value
var inputValue = $('#myInput').val();
console.log(inputValue);

// Setting a value
$('#myInput').val('New Input Value');
```

Conclusion

jQuery has transformed the way developers interact with the DOM, offering a rich API that streamlines many tasks associated with web development. Through its elegant methods for manipulating HTML content, modifying CSS, and managing attributes and properties, jQuery lets developers create dynamic, responsive user interfaces with ease.

By mastering these jQuery methods, you can take advantage of the library's capabilities to enhance your web applications. While modern JavaScript (ES6 and beyond) provides many of the features jQuery originally simplified, understanding these jQuery methods remains valuable, especially for legacy projects or when seeking rapid development solutions.

With this comprehensive guide, you are now equipped with a foundation for working with jQuery, enabling you to add interactive elements to your web projects effectively. Whether you are modifying content, styling elements, or managing form validations, jQuery's straightforward syntax and robust functionality open the door to efficient web development practices.

.

4. Events in jQuery

jQuery is a powerful JavaScript library that simplifies HTML document traversing, event handling, animating, and AJAX interactions for rapid web development. One of the core features of jQuery is its robust event handling capabilities, allowing developers to interact with user actions efficiently. This overview will delve into the basics of event handling in jQuery, discussing common events, event delegation, preventing default actions, and the creation of custom events.

Event Handling Basics

Event handling in jQuery revolves around the use of specific functions that respond to user interactions. This includes actions like clicking, hovering, typing, and more. The most fundamental function used for listening to events in jQuery is `.on()`. This method attaches one or more event handlers to the selected elements.

Syntax of `.on()`

```javascript
$(selector).on(event, childSelector, data, function)
```

- **selector**: The element(s) to bind the event to.
- **event**: A string representing the event type (e.g., "click").
- **childSelector**: Optional. If specified, the event handler is only applied to the child elements that match this selector.
- **data**: Optional. A data object passed to the event handler.
- **function**: The function to execute when the event is triggered.

Basic Example

Here is a simple example of binding a click event to a button:

```javascript
$(document).ready(function() {
   $('#myButton').on('click', function() {
      alert('Button was clicked!');
```

    });
});
```

In this example, when the button with the ID `myButton` is clicked, an alert box appears.

## Common jQuery Events

jQuery supports a wide range of events, allowing developers to handle various types of user interactions. Here are some of the most common jQuery events:

### Click Event

The click event is triggered when a user clicks on an element. It's one of the most frequently used events in web applications.

```javascript
$('#myButton').on('click', function() {
    console.log('Button clicked!');
});
```

Mouseover Event
```

The mouseover event occurs when the user moves the mouse pointer over an element. This event can be useful for providing visual feedback.

```javascript
$('#myElement').on('mouseover', function() {
    $(this).css('background-color', 'yellow');
});
```

Mouseout Event

Conversely, the mouseout event is triggered when the mouse pointer leaves the element. This event can be paired with mouseover to create hover effects.

```javascript
$('#myElement').on('mouseout', function() {
    $(this).css('background-color', '');
});
```

Keyup Event

The keyup event occurs when the user

releases a key on the keyboard. It can be used to capture user input in forms or search boxes.

```javascript
$('#myInput').on('keyup', function() {
    console.log('Input value: ' + $(this).val());
});
```

Focus and Blur Events

The focus event occurs when an element, such as an input field, gains keyboard focus. The blur event is triggered when the element loses focus.

```javascript
$('#myInput').on('focus', function() {
    $(this).css('bordcr', '2px solid blue');
}).on('blur', function() {
    $(this).css('border', '');
});
```

Event Delegation

Event delegation is a powerful technique in

jQuery that allows you to attach a single event handler to a parent element instead of multiple handlers to child elements. This is particularly useful for dynamically created elements, as it captures events bubbling up from child elements.

Why Use Event Delegation?

1. **Performance**: Attaching one event handler to a parent element is more efficient than attaching separate handlers to many child elements.

2. **Dynamic Content**: If child elements are added or removed after the event handler has been set up, the parent handler will still function without needing to re-bind events.

Example of Event Delegation

Here's an example of how to use event delegation to handle clicks on dynamically added list items:

```javascript
$(document).ready(function() {
```

```
$('#myList').on('click', 'li', function() {
    alert('Item clicked: ' + $(this).text());
});

// Adding a new item dynamically
$('#addItemButton').on('click', function() {
    $('#myList').append('<li>New Item</li>');
});
});
```

In this scenario, as new `<li>` elements are added, they can still be clicked, and the event handler will respond because it is attached to the parent `<ul>` element.

Preventing Default Actions

In many situations, developers may wish to prevent the default action associated with an event. For instance, clicking a link typically navigates to another page; you might want to prevent this behavior while still executing some JavaScript.

`preventDefault()`

To prevent the default action of an event, you can call the `event.preventDefault()` method within your event handler.

Example

Here's an example of preventing the default behavior of a hyperlink:

```javascript
$('a').on('click', function(event) {
    event.preventDefault(); // Prevents the browser from following the link
    alert('Link clicked, but navigation prevented!');
});
```

Custom Events

jQuery also allows developers to create and trigger their own custom events, which can be helpful for organizing your code and managing complex interactions.

Creating Custom Events

You can create a custom event using the `.trigger()` method, and then listen for it using `.on()`.

Example of Custom Events

Here's an example of how to create and handle a custom event:

```javascript
$(document).ready(function() {
   // Define a custom event
   $('#myElement').on('customEvent', function() {
      alert('Custom event triggered!');
   });

   // Trigger the custom event
   $('#triggerCustomEventButton').on('click', function() {
      $('#myElement').trigger('customEvent');
   });
});
```

In this example, when the button `#triggerCustomEventButton` is clicked, it triggers the custom event on `#myElement`, which in turn alerts the user.

Event handling in jQuery is a fundamental feature that enhances user interaction on web pages. Understanding basic and common events like click, mouseover, and keyup, along with concepts like event delegation, default action prevention, and custom event creation, provides developers with a powerful toolkit to build responsive and interactive applications. By effectively using these techniques, you can create a smoother and more engaging user experience on your websites.

Overall, mastering event handling in jQuery will significantly improve your ability to manage user interactions in web development.

5. jQuery Effects and Animations

jQuery, a popular JavaScript library, simplifies HTML document traversing, event handling, and animation for rapid web development. Its robust capabilities for creating effects and animations allow developers to enhance user experience and provide dynamic visual feedback that engages users. This comprehensive guide explores various jQuery effects and animations, including showing/hiding elements, fading, sliding, custom animations, and chaining effects and methods.

Show/Hide Effects

The show/hide effect is one of the most basic yet powerful functionalities provided by jQuery. These methods allow developers to dynamically display or conceal HTML elements with smooth transitions, enhancing the visual experience.

1. **`.show()`**
   - The `.show()` method is used to display the

hidden elements. By default, it sets the CSS display property to "block" (or inline block for inline elements).
  - Example:
    ```javascript
    $('#myElement').show();
    ```
  - This code snippet will make the element with the ID `myElement` visible immediately.

2. **`.hide()`**
  - Conversely, the `.hide()` method hides the specified elements by setting their display to "none".
  - Example:
    ```javascript
    $('#myElement').hide();
    ```
  - This will effectively remove `myElement` from the view.

3. **`.toggle()`**
  - The `.toggle()` method alternates the visibility of an element. If the element is visible, it hides it; if it is hidden, it shows it.
  - Example:
    ```javascript
    ```

```
$('#myElement').toggle();
```

- Use this method for user interactions, like showing additional content or toggling menus.

Fading Effects

Fading effects add a layer of sophistication. They transition an element's opacity, allowing it to appear and disappear smoothly rather than abruptly.

1. **`.fadeIn()`**
   - The `.fadeIn()` method gradually changes the opacity of the selected element from 0 to 1.
   - Example:
   ```javascript
   $('#myElement').fadeIn(1000); // Fades in over 1 second
   ```
   - This is useful for revealing elements slowly when they first appear on the page.

2. **`.fadeOut()`**
   - The `.fadeOut()` method transitions the opacity from 1 to 0, effectively hiding the

element.
  - Example:
  ```javascript
  $('#myElement').fadeOut(1000); // Fades out over 1 second
  ```

  - This method is commonly used for notifications or alerts that need to disappear after a short duration.

3. **`.fadeToggle()`**
  - The `.fadeToggle()` function combines both fadeIn and fadeOut in one method. It fades the element in if it's currently hidden and fades it out if it's currently shown.
  - Example:
  ```javascript
  $('#myElement').fadeToggle(500); // Fades in/out over 0.5 seconds
  ```

  - This method is perfect for creating interactive UI components like expanding menus.

Sliding Effects

Sliding animations provide a visual cue by

moving elements up or down on the page. This adds a fun and engaging way to show or hide sections of your layout.

1. **`.slideUp()`**
   - The `.slideUp()` method hides an element by sliding it upwards, reducing its height from its original size to zero.
   - Example:
     ```javascript
     $('#myElement').slideUp(1000); // Slides up over 1 second
     ```
   - It's typically used for collapsing sections, such as accordion panels.

2. **`.slideDown()`**
   - The `.slideDown()` method reveals an element by increasing its height from 0 to its full size, creating the appearance of the element sliding down.
   - Example:
     ```javascript
     $('#myElement').slideDown(1000); // Slides down over 1 second
     ```
   - This complements the slideUp effect

perfectly for showing previously hidden content.

3. **`.slideToggle()`**
   - Similar to `.toggle()`, the `.slideToggle()` method toggles the visibility of the selected elements with a sliding motion.
   - Example:
     ```javascript
     $('#myElement').slideToggle(500); // Slides up or down over 0.5 seconds
     ```
   - This is particularly useful for interactive interfaces, like dropdown menus.

Custom Animations with `.animate()`

jQuery's `.animate()` method allows for custom animations on numeric properties of CSS, such as `height`, `width`, `opacity`, and other applicable CSS attributes. This means developers can create nuanced animations beyond the basic effects.

- The syntax for `.animate()` is as follows:
  ```javascript
  $(element).animate({ properties }, duration,
```

easing, complete);
```

- Example:
```javascript
$('#myElement').animate({ height: 'toggle', opacity: 'toggle' }, 1000);
```
- In the above example, the element will toggle its height and opacity simultaneously over 1 second.

- Here, you can define various properties and their target values, making it straightforward to create complex animations. Options for easing can also be included, such as `linear` or `swing`, to control the acceleration over time.

Chaining Effects and Methods

Chaining is a fundamental feature in jQuery that allows multiple effects or methods to be applied sequentially to the same element. This can lead to cleaner, more efficient code and smoother animations.

- Chaining is done simply by calling multiple
```

methods one after the other on the same jQuery object.

Example:
```javascript
$('#myElement')
  .fadeIn(500)
  .slideDown(500)
  .animate({ opacity: 0.5 }, 500)
  .fadeOut(500);
```

In this example, the `#myElement` fades in over 0.5 seconds, slides down over another 0.5 seconds, animates its opacity to 0.5 over 0.5 seconds, and finally fades out again over another 0.5 seconds. The seamless transition between effects creates a polished and engaging experience for users.

Conclusion

jQuery effects and animations significantly enrich user interactions on websites. Mastering these methods, including show/hide effects, fading, sliding, custom animations with `.animate()`, and the ability to chain effects, provides developers with a robust toolset for enhancing the dynamic nature of web applications. By leveraging these features, developers can create visually appealing and user-friendly interfaces that captivate and engage their audience, resulting in improved usability and satisfaction. Whether you're building a simple website or a complex application, understanding and utilizing jQuery's animation capabilities is essential for crafting memorable user experiences.

6. AJAX with jQuery

Introduction to AJAX

Asynchronous JavaScript and XML (AJAX) is a set of web development techniques that allows web applications to communicate with a server asynchronously. This means that it enables web pages to update without requiring a full page reload. This capability enhances user experience by making web applications faster and more interactive. Although originally the term included XML, today, AJAX typically works with JSON (JavaScript Object Notation) due to its lightweight nature and easy integration with JavaScript.

AJAX applications can send and retrieve data without interfering with the display and behavior of the existing page. This is essential for providing smooth, dynamic content generation, such as loading new data when scrolling, updating user interfaces, and providing real-time notifications.

AJAX works well with jQuery, a fast, small, and feature-rich JavaScript library. jQuery simplifies HTML document traversing, event handling, animating, and Ajax interactions for rapid web development. When combined, AJAX and jQuery provide a powerful toolkit for creating dynamic applications that interact with server-side data seamlessly.

Making AJAX Requests with jQuery

With jQuery, making AJAX requests is straightforward and streamlined. The jQuery library provides several convenient methods to facilitate different types of AJAX operations:

`.ajax()`

The `.ajax()` method is the most versatile way to make AJAX requests. It allows you to customize every aspect of the request, including the URL, HTTP method, data type expected in response, and more. Here's a simple example of using `.ajax()` to retrieve data from a server:

```javascript
$.ajax({
```

```
    url: "https://api.example.com/data",
    type: "GET",
    dataType: "json",
    success: function(data) {
        console.log("Received data:", data);
    },
    error: function(jqXHR, textStatus, errorThrown) {
        console.error("Error fetching data:", textStatus, errorThrown);
    }
});
```

In this example:
- `url`: Specifies the resource from which to fetch the data.
- `type`: Defines the HTTP method (GET, POST, etc.).
- `dataType`: Indicates the type of data expected from the server (e.g., JSON, XML, HTML).
- `success`: A function that gets called when the request succeeds, receiving data as an argument.
- `error`: A function called when the request fails, providing error details for debugging.

`.get()`

For simpler GET requests, jQuery provides the `.get()` shorthand method, which is easier to write. Here's how you can achieve the same result using `.get()`:

```javascript
$.get("https://api.example.com/data", function(data) {
    console.log("Received data:", data);
}).fail(function(jqXHR, textStatus, errorThrown) {
    console.error("Error fetching data:", textStatus, errorThrown);
});
```

This example simplifies the AJAX call by eliminating the need for many parameters required in the `.ajax()` method.

`.post()`

Similarly, if you need to send data to the server, you can use the `.post()` method. It is often used for submitting forms. Here's an example:

```javascript
$.post("https://api.example.com/submit",
{ name: "John Doe", age: 30 },
function(response) {
   console.log("Server response:", response);
}).fail(function(jqXHR, textStatus, errorThrown) {
   console.error("Error submitting data:", textStatus, errorThrown);
});
```

In this case, the data payload (name and age) is sent to the server, with the server's response being logged if the request is successful.

Handling Responses

AJAX requests can return various types of data, and handling these responses effectively is crucial for an application's functionality. The success function provides a callback for handling successful responses, while error handling functions can manage any errors that arise during the request.

In a typical workflow, you may have different ways to handle various response codes. Here's an example to illustrate how to deal with successful and error responses:

```javascript
$.ajax({
   url: "https://api.example.com/user",
   type: "GET",
   dataType: "json",
   success: function(data) {
      // Process the received data
      $("#userName").text(data.name);
      $("#userEmail").text(data.email);
   },
   error: function(jqXHR) {
      if (jqXHR.status === 404) {
         console.error("User not found.");
      } else {
         console.error("Error:", jqXHR.statusText);
      }
   }
});
```

Working with JSON Data

JSON is widely used in modern web applications due to its simplicity and ease of use with JavaScript. When the server returns data in JSON format, jQuery automatically parses it for you if you set the `dataType` to "json", as shown in the previous examples.

Here's a deeper look at handling JSON data from an AJAX response:

Suppose the server responds with the following JSON object:

```json
{
   "id": 1,
   "name": "Alice",
   "email": "alice@example.com",
   "age": 28
}
```

You can handle this response in your success function as follows:

```javascript
$.get("https://api.example.com/user/1",
```

```
function(data) {
    const user = `
      <div>
        <h1>${data.name}</h1>
        <p>Email: ${data.email}</p>
        <p>Age: ${data.age}</p>
      </div>
    `;
    $("#userDetails").html(user);
}).fail(function(jqXHR, textStatus, errorThrown) {
    console.error("Error fetching user details:", textStatus, errorThrown);
});
```

Here, the user data is dynamically added to the HTML of your webpage, demonstrating the power of JSON in conjunction with AJAX and jQuery.

Error Handling in AJAX Requests

Error handling is an essential aspect of AJAX development. It helps in providing users with feedback when something goes wrong. When using jQuery's AJAX methods, you can use the `error` option to specify what to do in the event of an error.

If an AJAX request fails, it can be due to various reasons, such as:
- Network issues
- Server errors (like 404 Not Found or 500 Internal Server Error)
- CORS (Cross-Origin Resource Sharing) issues

Here's an example of comprehensive error handling:

```javascript
$.ajax({
   url: "https://api.example.com/resource",
   type: "GET",
   dataType: "json",
   success: function(data) {
      console.log("Data received:", data);
   },
   error: function(jqXHR, textStatus, errorThrown) {
      // Log the error message to console
      console.error("Error details:", {
         status: jqXHR.status,
```

```
        statusText: jqXHR.statusText,
        error: errorThrown
    });

    // Display a user-friendly message
    alert("An error occurred while fetching data. Please try again.");
  }
});
```

By logging error details and informing the user of the failure, you help maintain a good user experience, even in situations where things do go wrong.

AJAX is a powerful technique for creating dynamic and interactive web applications. When combined with jQuery, it becomes easy to make requests to a server, handle responses, work with JSON data, and implement effective error handling. Understanding and implementing these concepts will significantly enhance your web development skills and enable you to create engaging and responsive user experiences. By utilizing jQuery's AJAX methods effectively, developers can build applications that look and feel smooth, leading to higher user satisfaction and interaction with your website or web application.

7. jQuery Plugins: A Comprehensive Guide

jQuery is a fast, lightweight, and feature-rich JavaScript library that simplifies the process of handling HTML document traversal and manipulation, event handling, animation, and Ajax interactions. One of the greatest strengths of jQuery is its extensibility through plugins, allowing developers to enhance the library's capabilities and create a more interactive user experience. This extensive overview will delve into jQuery plugins: what they are, how to find and use them, how to create your own, and a review of some popular jQuery plugins.

What Are jQuery Plugins?

jQuery plugins are pieces of reusable code that extend jQuery's functionality beyond its core features. They provide pre-built methods that can be easily integrated into a web project, enabling developers to add complex behavior to their web applications without having to write extensive JavaScript code from scratch. Plugins can serve various functions, including but not limited to UI components, enhancements for form elements, and utilities for manipulating DOM elements.

The architecture of jQuery plugins is essentially built on the idea of encapsulating functionalities while still allowing the flexibility of customization. Plugins take advantage of jQuery's capabilities to work seamlessly with the jQuery object, enhancing it by adding new methods. A well-designed jQuery plugin will be user-friendly, easy to integrate, and well-documented.

How to Find and Use jQuery Plugins

Finding jQuery Plugins

1. **jQuery Plugin Registry**: One of the first places to look for plugins is the [jQuery Plugin Registry](https://plugins.jquery.com/), which catalogs various plugins submitted by the community. Here, developers can search through categories or use keywords to find plugins that cater to their specific needs.

2. **GitHub**: Many developers host their

jQuery plugins on GitHub. Searching repositories can yield a plethora of options, including popular and actively maintained plugins.

3. **Web Development Blogs and Tutorials**: Numerous blogs and online tutorials provide insights into specific plugins. They often showcase use cases and practical examples, which are great for discovering useful plugins.

4. **Code Snippet Libraries**: Websites like CodePen, jsFiddle, and others often host snippets that utilize jQuery plugins, which can also serve as a resource for finding plugins and seeing them in action.

Using jQuery Plugins

Integrating a jQuery plugin into a project typically involves the following steps:

1. **Include jQuery**: Since plugins are built on top of jQuery, ensure that you include the jQuery library in your HTML file before any plugins.

```html
<script src="https://code.jquery.com/jquery-3.6.0.min.js"></script>
```

2. **Include the Plugin**: Download the plugin file (often a `.js` file) from the source, or link to it directly if it's hosted online.

```html
<script src="path/to/plugin.js"></script>
```

3. **Initialize the Plugin**: After including jQuery and the plugin file, you can initialize the plugin on a specific DOM element using jQuery selectors.

```javascript
$(document).ready(function(){
    $('#myElement').pluginName(options);
});
```

4. **Interactions and Customization**: Many plugins come with options for customization. Make sure to look at the documentation to

understand how to modify settings or respond to events.

Example of Using a jQuery Plugin

Here's a short example of how to use the popular jQuery plugin called Slick, a responsive carousel slider.

First, include jQuery and the Slick plugin in your HTML:

```html
<link rel="stylesheet" type="text/css" href="path/to/slick.css"/>
<script src="https://code.jquery.com/jquery-3.6.0.min.js"></script>
<script src="path/to/slick.min.js"></script>
```

Next, create an element to hold the images:

```html
<div class="your-slider">
   <div><img src="image1.jpg" alt="Image 1"></div>
   <div><img src="image2.jpg" alt="Image
```

2"></div>
   <div><img src="image3.jpg" alt="Image 3"></div>
</div>
```

Finally, initialize the Slick slider in your JavaScript:

```javascript
$(document).ready(function(){
   $('.your-slider').slick({
      setting1: value1,
      setting2: value2,
   });
});
```

Creating Your Own jQuery Plugin

Creating a jQuery plugin allows developers to encapsulate functionality that they can reuse across multiple projects. Below are the steps to create a simple jQuery plugin.

Step 1: Define the Plugin
```

Plugins are typically defined by extending the jQuery prototype object. This allows the plugin to be called as a method on any jQuery object.

```javascript
(function($){
   $.fn.myPlugin = function(options) {
      // Default settings
      var settings = $.extend({
         color: 'blue',
         fontSize: '14px'
      }, options);

      return this.each(function() {
         // Plugin code goes here
         $(this).css({
            color: settings.color,
            fontSize: settings.fontSize
         });
      });
   };
}(jQuery));
```

Step 2: Usage

To use your plugin, simply call it on a jQuery object, passing any custom options if needed.

```javascript
$(document).ready(function(){
   $('p').myPlugin({
      color: 'red',
      fontSize: '20px'
   });
});
```

Step 3: Testing and Documentation

Ensure that the plugin is thoroughly tested across different browsers and devices. Additionally, provide clear documentation to explain how to use the plugin, the options available, and any events that can be triggered.

Popular jQuery Plugins

While there are myriad jQuery plugins available, some have gained popularity due to their utility, ease of use, and active maintenance. Here are a few notable examples:

jQuery UI

[jQuery UI](https://jqueryui.com/) is a robust library that adds interaction and animation to your web applications. It integrates well with the core jQuery library, providing ready-to-use components such as:

- **Draggable**: Enables elements to be dragged and moved.
- **Droppable**: Sets up drop targets for draggable elements.
- **Accordion**: Collapsible sections that help organize content.
- **Datepicker**: A nice calendar picker for selecting dates.

jQuery UI makes web development easier by providing a consistent interface for these common UI tasks.

Slick

[Slick](https://kenwheeler.github.io/slick/) is a fully responsive carousel slider that is easy to implement and customize. It features:

- Infinite looping of slides.
- Variable width support.
- Lazy loading of images.
- Autoplay functionality.

Slick has become a favorite among developers for its flexibility and ease of use.

Select2

[Select2](https://select2.org/) is an enhancement for select boxes that improves usability. Some of its key features include:

- Searching among options for easier data retrieval.
- Support for tagging and selection of multiple options.
- Thematic styling and customization.

Select2 provides a better way to work with select inputs, especially when dealing with a large number of options.

Lightbox

[Lightbox] (https://lokeshdhakar.com/projects/lightbox2/) is a simple script to overlay images on the current page. Responsive and minimalistic, Lightbox allows for creating a photographic gallery experience.

Conclusion

jQuery plugins provide a powerful method to enhance functionality and expand the usability of web applications. They allow developers to integrate complex features with minimal effort, fostering a collaborative and efficient coding environment. Whether you are utilizing popular existing plugins or considering creating your own, jQuery plugins open up numerous possibilities for rich web experiences. With this guide, you should now be equipped with the essential knowledge about jQuery plugins, enabling you to leverage them effectively in your projects.

8. Introduction to jQuery UI

jQuery UI is a powerful set of user interface components built on top of the jQuery library. It provides developers with an assortment of customizable, reusable interface elements that simplify the process of creating rich, interactive web applications. Whether you need to implement complex interactions like drag-and-drop or integrate components like sliders, accordions, or datepickers, jQuery UI has you covered.

jQuery UI also facilitates the design of responsive and user-friendly layouts, making it easier for developers to create applications that work seamlessly across different devices. It is particularly useful for those who want to enhance their web applications without delving into the complexities of creating UI components from scratch.

Using jQuery UI Components

One of the primary advantages of jQuery UI is its wide array of pre-built UI components.

Here, we'll cover several essential components, including the accordion, dialog, and datepicker.

Accordion

The accordion widget allows developers to create collapsible content sections. This is especially useful for organizing content and saving screen space.

To implement an accordion, you first need the HTML structure, which usually consists of a series of headings and associated panels:

```html
<div id="accordion">
  <h3>Section 1</h3>
  <div>
    <p>Content for Section 1.</p>
  </div>
  <h3>Section 2</h3>
  <div>
    <p>Content for Section 2.</p>
  </div>
</div>
```

After including the necessary jQuery and jQuery UI scripts in your HTML, you can initialize the accordion with the following jQuery code:

```javascript
$( function() {
    $( "#accordion" ).accordion({
        heightStyle: "content" // Automatically adjusts the height of the panels
    });
});
```

Dialog

The dialog widget is another essential UI component that allows developers to create modal or non-modal dialog boxes. Dialogs are useful for alert messages, confirmations, or form inputs.

Here's how to implement a simple dialog:

```html
<div id="dialog" title="Dialog Title">
  <p>This is a dialog box!</p>
```

```
</div>
```

You can initialize the dialog using jQuery like this:

```javascript
$( function() {
   $( "#dialog" ).dialog({
      autoOpen: false, // Prevents the dialog from opening immediately
      modal: true // Makes the dialog modal
   });

   // Open the dialog when the user clicks a button
   $( "#open-dialog" ).on("click", function() {
      $( "#dialog" ).dialog( "open" );
   });
});
```

Datepicker

The datepicker widget is particularly helpful for allowing users to select dates, ensuring that date input is standardized and easy to manage.

You can implement a datepicker as follows:

```html
<p>Date: <input type="text" id="datepicker"></p>
```

Then initialize the datepicker with:

```javascript
$( function() {
   $( "#datepicker" ).datepicker();
});
```

The datepicker can also be customized with options such as date formats and the range of selectable dates.

Theming with jQuery UI

One of the most appealing aspects of jQuery UI is its flexible theming. By using the jQuery UI ThemeRoller, developers can easily create a custom theme that goes along with their application's design.

Using ThemeRoller

ThemeRoller is a web-based tool that allows you to design and download a theme for jQuery UI. You can customize various aspects of your theme, including colors, icon styles, and fonts. Once you have your theme designed:

- Download the CSS files generated by ThemeRoller.
- Include those CSS files in your HTML document.

```html
<link rel="stylesheet" href="path_to_your_custom_theme.css">
```

After including your custom theme, all jQuery UI components will reflect the new styling, allowing for a cohesive design.

Customizing Widgets

You may also directly customize the appearance of individual components using CSS. jQuery UI components come with specific classes that you can target to override default styles. For instance, if you want to change the font color of all buttons:

```css
.ui-button {
    color: #ff0000; /* Changes text color to red */
}
```

By leveraging custom styles alongside ThemeRoller, you can achieve a unique look for your application that stands out from default jQuery UI themes.

Customizing and Creating New Interactions

jQuery UI not only provides a collection of built-in components but also allows developers to create custom interactions. By utilizing the extensive options available in the jQuery UI API, developers can tailor the behavior of existing components or even create entirely new ones.

Creating Custom Interactions

jQuery UI enables the creation of custom interactions through the use of the interactions API. You can leverage built-in interactions such as draggable, droppable, and sortable to enhance your application.

Example: Custom Draggable and Droppable

Suppose you want to create a simple drag-and-drop feature where users can drag an item into a designated drop zone. Here's how you might set that up:

HTML structure:

```html
<div id="draggable" class="ui-widget-content">
  <p>Drag me!</p>
</div>
```

```html
<div id="droppable" class="ui-widget-header">
  <p>Drop here</p>
</div>
```

jQuery initialization:

```javascript
$( function() {
    $( "#draggable" ).draggable(); // Make the element draggable
    $( "#droppable" ).droppable({
        drop: function( event, ui ) {
            $( this )
                .addClass( "ui-state-highlight" )
                .find( "p" )
                    .html( "Dropped!" );
        }
    });
});
```

In this example, when the draggable element is dropped into the droppable zone, the CSS class `ui-state-highlight` is added, providing visual feedback to users.

Custom Widget Creation

If the provided components and interactions are not sufficient for your needs, you can also create custom widgets. This involves extending the jQuery UI widget factory, which allows you to define new components with their own methods, options, and events. Here's a simple example of a custom widget:

```javascript
$.widget("custom.myWidget", {
   options: {
      color: "blue"
   },

   _create: function() {
      this.element.css("color", this.options.color);
      this._on(this.element, {
         click: "changeColor"
      });
   },

   changeColor: function() {
      this.element.css("color", this.element.css("color") === "blue" ? "red" :
```

```
"blue");
    }
});

// Usage
$( function() {
    $( "#myElement" ).myWidget(); // Initialize the custom widget
});
```

In this example, a new widget named `myWidget` is created that toggles the text color between blue and red upon clicking.

Conclusion

jQuery UI represents a comprehensive solution for developing rich user interfaces in web applications. With its wide range of pre-built components, strong theming capabilities, and flexibility for custom interactions and widgets, it allows developers to focus more on functionality and user experience rather than worrying about intricacies of UI implementation.

By leveraging the power of jQuery UI, developers can ensure that their applications are not only functional but also visually appealing and user-friendly. Whether you're building a simple website or a complex web application, jQuery UI is equipped to meet your needs, making it a valuable tool in the web development ecosystem.

9.Performance Optimization in jQuery

When developing web applications, ensuring that your code runs efficiently is crucial. Poorly optimized code can lead to slow performance, increased load times, and a negative user experience. jQuery, though powerful and widely used, can sometimes introduce performance bottlenecks if not used wisely. In this extensive discussion, we will explore best practices for writing efficient jQuery code, focusing on minimizing DOM manipulation, leveraging event delegation, and reducing jQuery load times.

Best Practices for Writing Efficient jQuery Code

To harness the full potential of jQuery while maintaining performance, developers should adhere to several best practices:

1. **Use the Latest Version**: Always make sure you are using the latest stable version of jQuery. Each release includes performance optimizations and bug fixes that can enhance

your application's speed and reliability.

2. **Minimize Selectors**: jQuery selectors can be costly in terms of performance. Avoid complex selectors and instead use IDs or classes that are specific to the elements you want to target. For example, prefer `$('#myId')` over `$('.class .child')`. When more specific selectors are needed, make sure they target the simplest path possible to minimize the search time.

3. **Chain Methods**: jQuery allows method chaining, which can significantly reduce the performance overhead associated with multiple DOM queries. Instead of calling `$('.myElement1').addClass('active'); $('.myElement2').hide();`, you can chain the methods: `$('.myElement1').addClass('active').end().hide();`. This approach reduces the amount of repeated DOM traversal and manipulation.

4. **Cache jQuery Objects**: When working with the same jQuery object multiple times, store it in a variable instead of querying the DOM repeatedly. For instance, rather than

using `$('.myClass')` multiple times, you can cache this selector:

```javascript
var $myElements = $('.myClass');
$myElements.addClass('active');
$myElements.hide();
```

5. **Avoid Inline Styles**: Modifying inline styles via jQuery can be less efficient. Instead, manipulate CSS classes. This practice not only enhances performance but also improves maintainability and readability by centralizing style definitions in CSS files. Use `addClass()`, `removeClass()`, and `toggleClass()` instead of directly setting styles with `.css()`.

Minimizing DOM Manipulation

DOM manipulation is one of the most significant performance impacts in web applications. Here are several strategies to minimize it effectively:

1. **Batch Changes**: Rather than making individual changes to the DOM for every

update, batch them together. If you need to add several items to a list, create the new items as a string and then append them to the DOM in one operation. For instance:

```javascript
var items = '';
for (var i = 0; i < 100; i++) {
    items += '<li>' + i + '</li>';
}
$('#myList').append(items);
```

2. **Use Document Fragments**: When you manipulate a large number of DOM elements, consider using a `DocumentFragment`. You can create a fragment, populate it, and then append it to the DOM in one go. This approach significantly reduces rendering time because the browser does not have to reflow or repaint every time an element is added:

```javascript
var fragment = document.createDocumentFragment();
for (var i = 0; i < 100; i++) {
    var li = document.createElement('li');
    li.textContent = i;
    fragment.appendChild(li);
```

}

   document.getElementById('myList').appendChild(fragment);
   ```

3. **Visibility Alteration Techniques**: When working with elements that need to be displayed or hidden, use `visibility` and `opacity` instead of `display` when possible. Changing the `display` property causes reflow and repaint, whereas `visibility` and `opacity` changes do not.

4. **Remove Elements from the DOM When Not Needed**: If an element is not required anymore, remove it from the DOM rather than keeping it invisible. Keeping unnecessary elements can add to the memory footprint and slow down the rendering of necessary items.

5. **Debounce or Throttle Resize and Scroll Events**: If you are attaching event handlers to `resize` or `scroll`, consider debounce or throttle techniques to limit how often your functions are fired. For instance, using a 100ms delay allows the function to execute
   ```

once, even if the event occurs multiple times during that duration:

```javascript
var timeout;
$(window).on('resize', function() {
  clearTimeout(timeout);
  timeout = setTimeout(function() {
    // Your resize functions here
  }, 100);
});
```

Using Event Delegation Wisely

Event delegation allows you to simplify event handling by taking advantage of event bubbling. Instead of attaching an event handler to every element individually, you can attach it to a parent element. This approach reduces memory usage and improves performance, especially for dynamic content.

1. **Delegate Events to a Parent**: Instead of binding events to individual items, bind events to a shared parent and handle the events in a single function:
  ```javascript
  ```

```
$('#parent').on('click', '.child', function() {
    // Handle click event for .child elements
});
```

2. **Careful Use of `.on()`**: With jQuery's `on()` method, you can achieve both event delegation and dynamic element binding. This is especially useful for elements added to the DOM after the initial binding. Using `on()` allows newly created child elements to automatically take part in the bound event without extra event binding.

3. **Limit Delegation to Relevant Elements**: While event delegation is powerful, be mindful to limit the selectors to the relevant elements to avoid unnecessary event triggering and handling. Too broad of a parent selector can lead to performance issues, especially if it contains many child elements.

Reducing jQuery Load Times

Optimizing jQuery load times is crucial to enhancing the overall performance of your web application. Here are some effective strategies:

1. **Minification**: Ensure you are using a minified version of jQuery. This reduces the file size and minimizes the time it takes for the file to download. You can find minified versions on jQuery's official website.

2. **Serve from a CDN**: Utilize a Content Delivery Network (CDN) to host your jQuery files. CDNs often have faster servers and can cache the library across different websites. If a user has already visited a site using the same version of jQuery from the same CDN, it will load instantly from their cache.

3. **Load jQuery Asynchronously**: If jQuery isn't needed until after the page is fully loaded, you can load it asynchronously. This can be done by including the script at the end of the `<body>` or using the `async` attribute:
   ```html
   <script src="https://code.jquery.com/jquery-3.6.0.min.js" async></script>
   ```

4. **Combine and Minify Scripts**: If you

are using multiple JavaScript files along with jQuery, consider combining them into a single file and minifying that file. This reduces the number of HTTP requests, leading to faster load times.

5. **Defer Non-Critical Scripts**: For scripts that are not critical for the initial user experience, employ the `defer` attribute to ensure that they execute after the HTML document has been fully parsed.
```html
<script src="your-script.js" defer></script>
```

Optimizing jQuery performance involves a careful balance between efficient coding practices and strategic decisions on how we handle DOM interactions and script loading. By adhering to the best practices outlined in this discussion, developers can significantly improve the efficiency of their jQuery code, resulting in faster load times, quicker response times, and an overall better user experience. By minimizing DOM manipulation, leveraging event delegation, and reducing jQuery load times, web applications can harness the power of jQuery while maintaining peak performance.

10. Debugging and Troubleshooting jQuery

Debugging and troubleshooting are crucial skills for any developer, particularly when working with libraries like jQuery. These tools can simplify JavaScript development, but they also come with their own set of challenges. In this guide, we'll explore common jQuery errors, how to use developer tools effectively for debugging, and best practices for troubleshooting jQuery code.

Common jQuery Errors and How to Fix Them

1. **Uncaught TypeError: $(...).xxx is not a function**
This error typically occurs when jQuery is not loaded correctly or when the jQuery variable `$` is being overwritten by another JavaScript library.

Fix:
- Ensure jQuery is loaded correctly in your HTML file. Check the `<script>` tags for correct paths and ensure it is included before

any jQuery code executes.
- Use `jQuery.noConflict()` if you are using another library that uses `$`. This method prevents conflicts by allowing you to use jQuery with a different variable.

```javascript
jQuery.noConflict();
jQuery(document).ready(function($) {
    // Your jQuery code here
});
```

2. **Uncaught ReferenceError: $ is not defined**
This error implies that jQuery hasn't been loaded before its usage in your script.

Fix:
- Ensure your jQuery script tag is placed before your custom JavaScript code. It is best practice to place all `<script>` tags just before the closing `</body>` tag to ensure that all HTML elements have been loaded.

3. **Element not found**
You might encounter this issue when using a

selector that doesn't match any element in the DOM. Errors like `Uncaught TypeError: Cannot read property 'xxx' of null` indicate that jQuery cannot find an element to work with.

Fix:
- Double-check your selectors. Always ensure that the elements you're trying to interact with exist in the DOM.
- Wrap your jQuery code in a `$(document).ready()` function to ensure that the code executes only after the DOM is fully loaded.

```javascript
$(document).ready(function() {
    // Safely interact with DOM elements here
});
```

4. **Events not triggering**
Sometimes, you might set up event handlers, but the events do not trigger as expected.

Fix:
- Make sure to use event delegation if

dynamically inserting elements into the DOM. For example, if you are adding a button after the page loads, your original event binding on that button will not work unless it's done on an existing parent element. Use `.on()` for delegation:

```javascript
$(document).on('click', '.dynamic-button', function() {
   // Event code here
});
```

5. **Animations and transitions not working**
A common issue is when animations or transitions fail to trigger, often with no visible error.

Fix:
- Check CSS for conflicts. Ensure that styles on the target elements are not set in a way that prevents visibility or relaxations.
- Debug using `console.log`, and make sure the animations are actually being called.

```javascript
$('.element').fadeIn(1000, function() {
   console.log("Fade completed.");
});
```

Using Developer Tools for Debugging

Modern browsers come equipped with powerful developer tools, making debugging JavaScript and jQuery easier. Here's how to leverage these tools:

1. **Console**
The console is your first stop for diagnosing issues. Use `console.log()` to output variable values or to indicate whether certain portions of your code are executing.

```javascript
console.log("Debugging: ", variableName);
```

You can also use the console for evaluating and executing JavaScript commands directly in the context of your open webpage.

2. **Breakpoints**
In the Sources tab of developer tools, you can set breakpoints to pause script execution and inspect the current state of variables or DOM elements. Breakpoints can be set on specific lines of your code, allowing you to step through your JavaScript line-by-line.

3. **Inspecting Elements**
Using the Elements tab lets you inspect your HTML structure and the associated styles. You can modify elements on-the-fly to see how your jQuery code might react to different structures.

4. **Network Tab**
The Network tab can be invaluable for understanding AJAX calls made by your jQuery code. It allows you to inspect responses, statuses, and the time taken for requests.

5. **Error Messages**
The console will display errors related to your jQuery, which provide insights into what went wrong. Click on the error message to navigate directly to the line in the code that triggered

the error.

Best Practices for Troubleshooting jQuery Code

1. **Use `$(document).ready()`**
Always wrap your jQuery code in the `$(document).ready()` function to ensure it runs after the DOM is fully loaded. This reduces issues related to manipulating elements that are not yet present.

2. **Leverage `console.log()` generously**
Before you start applying changes to your code, use `console.log()` strategically to understand the flow of your code. It's a simple yet powerful way to output data to the console.

3. **Comment out sections of code**
If you're uncertain where the issue is occurring, systematically comment out sections of your code. This will help isolate the problem area.

4. **Use jQuery's built-in methods**

Instead of relying solely on traditional JavaScript methods, utilize jQuery methods for DOM manipulation and event handling. They are built to handle cross-browser inconsistencies.

5. **Check for jQuery conflicts**
If your script is behaving unexpectedly, consider whether another library is conflicting. Check for other libraries that might be using the `$` variable. Use `jQuery.noConflict()` in such cases.

6. **Modularize your code**
Break your code into smaller functions or modules. This will not only make the code cleaner but will also make debugging specific portions easier. Each function can be tested independently.

7. **Ensure proper error handling**
Use try-catch blocks to handle exceptions gracefully. This can prevent your entire script from failing due to an unhandled error.

```javascript
try {
```

```
  // Code that might throw an error
} catch (e) {
  console.error("An error occurred: ", e);
}
```

Debugging and troubleshooting in jQuery can be daunting, but with the right approaches and tools, these tasks become manageable. By understanding common errors, effectively utilizing browser developer tools, and adhering to best practices, you can significantly enhance the reliability of your jQuery code. Remember that debugging is a natural part of development; embracing it can lead you to become a more proficient developer.

11. Migrating to jQuery Versions: A Comprehensive Guide

As web development continues to evolve, libraries like jQuery play a significant role in simplifying DOM manipulation, event handling, and Ajax interactions. However, with each new release, jQuery introduces optimizations, new features, and occasionally, breaking changes that can challenge developers when migrating from older versions. This guide aims to provide an in-depth understanding of the differences between jQuery versions, a step-by-step process for migrating to the latest version, and crucial information regarding deprecated methods and their alternatives.

Understanding Version Differences

jQuery uses a versioning system that includes three parts: major, minor, and patch (e.g., 3.6.0). Each part serves a specific purpose:

1. **Major Version**: Changes in this version indicate breaking changes, potentially

affecting code compatibility. For example, moving from jQuery 1.x to 2.x or 3.x usually requires careful attention to deprecated features and methods, as these versions may remove functionality present in earlier versions.

2. **Minor Version**: A change here typically adds new functionalities or improvements but does not introduce breaking changes. While often safe to implement, it's still recommended to review the release notes for any slight behavioral modifications.

3. **Patch Version**: These versions fix bugs and may include performance improvements. Generally, upgrading to a new patch version within the same major version is straightforward.

Migrating from Older jQuery Versions to the Latest

Migrating older jQuery versions (such as 1.x or 2.x) to the latest version (3.x) can present challenges, but a structured approach can simplify the process. Here's a step-by-step guide to ensure a smooth transition:

Step 1: Review Release Notes

Before initiating a migration, thoroughly read through jQuery's release notes for each version leading up to the target version. The notes often contain critical information on:

- New features
- Deprecated methods
- Changes in behavior for existing methods

As an example, jQuery 3.x deprecated certain features which were common in earlier versions, such as `$.ajaxSetup` or `.size()`. Understanding these will better prepare you to adapt your code accordingly.

Step 2: Audit Your Current jQuery Usage

Conduct an audit of your existing codebase to identify the usage of jQuery methods and functions. This involves:

- Searching for the `jQuery` and `$` keywords

- Listing all methods used
- Highlighting any deprecated methods

Tools like jQuery Migrate can assist in this phase by highlighting potential issues in your code when an older version of jQuery is running alongside the latest version.

Step 3: Update jQuery Version

Once sufficient review and preparation are completed, update your jQuery version in the project. You can do this by:

- Downloading the latest version from [jQuery's official site](https://jquery.com/download/)
- Updating the `<script>` reference in your HTML

Consider using a CDN for easier management and better performance:

```html
<script src="https://ajax.googleapis.com/ajax/libs/jquery/3.6.0/jquery.min.js"></script>
```

```

#### Step 4: Test Your Application

After updating, execute thorough testing to identify any issues:

- Run unit tests if available.
- Test all critical features to ensure that functionality remains intact.
- Check the browser console for warnings related to deprecated features.

### Deprecated Methods and Their Alternatives

As jQuery has evolved, several methods and functionalities have been marked as deprecated, leading to potential breakpoints in older applications. Here are some notable deprecated methods along with their alternatives:

1. **`.size()` Method**
   - **Deprecated**: The `.size()` method has been deprecated as it simply returns the length of a jQuery object.
```

- **Alternative**: Use `.length` property directly on the jQuery object.
```javascript
// Old way
var count = $("div").size();

// New way
var count = $("div").length;
```

2. **`.bind()`, `.unbind()`, `.delegate()`, and `.undelegate()`**
   - **Deprecated**: These methods were used for binding and unbinding event handlers.
   - **Alternative**: Use `.on()` for binding and `.off()` for unbinding events.
```javascript
// Old way
$(".myClass").bind("click", function() { /*...*/ });

// New way
$(".myClass").on("click", function() { /*...*/ });
```

3. **`.load()`, `.unload()`, and `.error()`**

- **Deprecated**: These methods were primarily used for handling events when content is loaded, unloaded, or when an error occurs.
- **Alternative**: Use `.on()` method with specific event types.

```javascript
// Old way
$("#myElement").load("ajax/test.html");

// New way
$.get("ajax/test.html", function(data) {
   $("#myElement").html(data);
});
```

4. **`.is(":visible")`**
   - **Deprecated**: This pseudo-selector has been deprecated in jQuery 3.x.
   - **Alternative**: Use `.css("display")` to check visibility.

```javascript
// Old way
if ($("#myElement").is(":visible")) { /*...*/ }

// New way
```

```js
if ($("#myElement").css("display") !== "none") { /*...*/ }
```

5. **`.ajaxSetup()`**
   - **Deprecated**: Though still operational, its use has decreased due to more nuanced approaches to configuring Ajax requests.
   - **Alternative**: Use global settings with `$.ajax()` for greater control and modern usage.

```javascript
// Old way
$.ajaxSetup({ cache: false });

// New way
$.ajax({ url: 'example.com', cache: false });
```

Migrating to the latest version of jQuery can appear daunting, especially when tackling older code. However, with a systematic approach of reviewing changes, auditing current usage, testing your application, and adapting to new standards, developers can ensure that their applications continue to perform efficiently while leveraging the improvements in performance and functionality that newer versions offer.

By staying informed about deprecated methods and embracing their alternatives, developers can not only enhance their applications but also keep their codebase up-to-date and easier to maintain in the long run. Following this guide will empower you to make smart decisions for your next jQuery migration, ensuring your web applications remain cutting-edge and robust.

12. Example: Simple To-Do List Application using jQuery

Step 1: Set Up the HTML Structure

Create a file named `index.html` and include the following HTML code:

```html
<!DOCTYPE html>
<html lang="en">
<head>
    <meta charset="UTF-8">
    <meta name="viewport" content="width=device-width, initial-scale=1.0">
    <title>Simple To-Do List</title>
    <link rel="stylesheet" href="styles.css">
    <script src="https://code.jquery.com/jquery-3.6.0.min.js"></script> <!-- Include jQuery -->
</head>
<body>
    <div class="container">
        <h1>To-Do List</h1>
```

```html
    <input type="text" id="taskInput" placeholder="Add a new task...">
    <button id="addTaskButton">Add Task</button>
    <ul id="taskList"></ul>
  </div>

  <script src="script.js"></script> <!-- Include jQuery script -->
</body>
</html>
```

Step 2: Style the Application

Create a file named `styles.css` and add some basic styles:

```css
body {
    font-family: Arial, sans-serif;
    background-color: #f4f4f4;
}

.container {
    width: 300px;
    margin: 50px auto;
```

```css
  padding: 20px;
  background: #fff;
  box-shadow: 0 0 10px rgba(0, 0, 0, 0.1);
}

h1 {
  text-align: center;
}

input {
  width: calc(100% - 40px);
  padding: 10px;
  margin-bottom: 10px;
}

button {
  padding: 10px;
  cursor: pointer;
}

ul {
  list-style-type: none;
  padding: 0;
}

li {
  padding: 10px;
```

```
    background: #e2e2e2;
    margin: 5px 0;
    position: relative;
}

.removeTask {
    position: absolute;
    right: 10px;
    cursor: pointer;
    color: red;
}
```

Step 3: Create the jQuery Script

Create a file named `script.js` and add the following jQuery code:

```javascript
$(document).ready(function() {
    // Function to add a new task
    $('#addTaskButton').click(function() {
        var taskText = $('#taskInput').val();

        if (taskText) {
            $('#taskList').append('<li>' + taskText + ' <span
```

```
class="removeTask">X</span></li>');
        $('#taskInput').val(''); // Clear the input field
    } else {
        alert('Please enter a task.');
    }
});

    // Event delegation to remove a task
    $('#taskList').on('click', '.removeTask', function() {
        $(this).parent().remove(); // Remove the entire list item
    });
});
```

Step 4: Run Your Application

Open the `index.html` file in your web browser. You should see a simple to-do list application. Here's how it works:

1. **Adding a Task**:
   - Type a task into the input field and click the "Add Task" button.
   - The task will appear in the list below with

a button (X) to remove it.

2. **Removing a Task**:
   - Click the (X) next to a task to remove it from the list.

You have now created a simple jQuery application for managing a to-do list. This example demonstrates how to manipulate the DOM using jQuery, handle events, and manage user inputs effectively. You can further expand upon this application by adding features such as saving tasks to local storage, editing tasks, or marking them as completed.

Index

1. Introduction to jQuery pg.4

2. Basic Concepts in jQuery pg.14

3. Working with jQuery: An In-Depth Exploration of DOM Manipulation and CSS Modification pg.24

4. Events in jQuery pg.35

5. jQuery Effects and Animations pg.45

6. AJAX with jQuery pg.54

7. jQuery Plugins: A Comprehensive Guide pg.65

8.Introduction to jQuery UI pg.76

9.Performance Optimization in jQuery pg.88

10.Debugging and Troubleshooting jQuery pg.98

11.Migrating to jQuery Versions: A Comprehensive Guide pg.107

12.Example: Simple To-Do List Application using jQuery pg.116

www.ingramcontent.com/pod-product-compliance
Lightning Source LLC
Chambersburg PA
CBHW050310230526
45471CB00005B/2111